Many blessings

14:6

50

D0855822

the Butterfly

the miracle of
spiritual rebirth

B^{the}utterfly

the miracle of
spiritual rebirth

Lucille Deith

SQUAREONE
PUBLISHERS

COVER DESIGNERS: Phaedra Mastrocola, Jacqueline Michelus, and Jeannie Tudor
COVER PHOTOGRAPH: Getty Images, Inc.
INTERIOR PHOTOGRAPHS: Lucille Deith
INTERIOR DESIGNER: Jacqueline Michelus
EDITORS: Amy Tecklenberg and Marie Caratozzolo

Square One Publishers
115 Herricks Road • Garden City Park, NY 11040
www.squareonepublishers.com • (516) 535–2010 • (866) 900-BOOK

Permission Credits
Scripture passages are taken from *Holy Bible, New International Version.*
Copyright © 1973, 1978, 1984 by International Bible Society.
Used by permission of Zondervan Publishing House. All rights reserved.

Cataloging-in-Publication Data
Deith, Lucille.
   The butterfly : the miracle of spiritual rebirth / Lucille Deith.
      p. cm.
   ISBN 0-7570-0258-7
1. Regeneration (Theology)–Miscellanea. 2. Butterflies–Metamorphosis–
Miscellanea. I. Title.

BT790.D35 2005
248–dc22

                                                    2005001218

Printed in Singapore

10 9 8 7 6 5 4 3 2 1

Contents

I lovingly dedicate this book to
my beautiful granddaughter,
Deanna.
Without her, this book would
not have materialized.
She has a vibrant smile and
a heart for Jesus.
She is my shining star.

Acknowledgments

This entire book was God-inspired. It was His love, wisdom, and guidance that made it possible for me to complete it. The many miraculous ways it all developed could only have been through His power. I pray it will accomplish all He intended for it to do, as it was written for His glory.

I also want to thank my many Christian sisters for their encouragement and their excitement for me. May God bless all of you.

Also, many thanks to Square One Publishers and its staff for seeing a vision beyond my expectations.

In the beginning
God created the heavens and the earth.
He created all living things.
Among the many creatures He created
was the beautiful butterfly.
And God saw that it was good.

1

A Butterfly

They flutter low and sail so high,
They rest on flowers and kiss the sky.
They sail through the air with graceful ease.
Land on my hand, "Oh, would you, please?"
Their colors so vibrant and markings unique,
I shudder with joy as one brushes my cheek.
A caterpillar no more as you flutter by,
Born again, a butterfly.

The Caterpillar

A butterfly begins its life as a caterpillar.
It eats everything in its path, trying to be
filled. But nothing can satisfy its hunger.

Just as *we* live and try many things
to fill *our* hunger. But nothing can fill us.

There is always that empty space,
that void–until we find Jesus.

A monarch butterfly
caterpillar looking
for a resting place.

4

The Chrysalis

Then the caterpillar goes into a chrysalis and rests. It just rests in the Lord and trusts Him to finish the good work He has begun.

As the caterpillar allows God to mold it into something beautiful, so must *we* rest in Him, and allow Him to do a good work in us.

> . . . BEING CONFIDENT OF THIS, THAT
> HE WHO BEGAN A GOOD WORK IN YOU
> WILL CARRY IT ON TO COMPLETION
> UNTIL THE DAY OF CHRIST JESUS.
>
> PHILIPPIANS 1:6

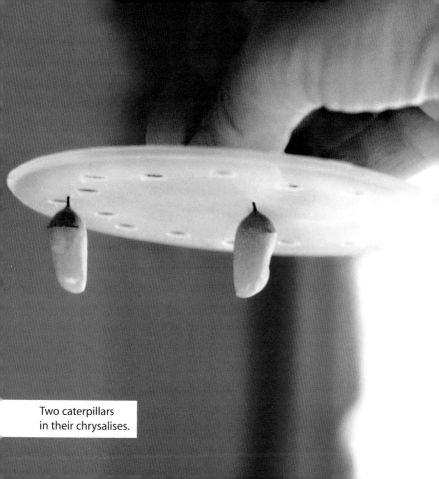

Two caterpillars
in their chrysalises.

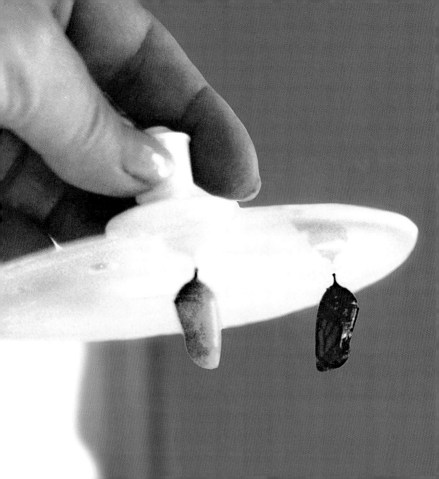

Within the chrysalis, the caterpillar starts to change and transform into a beautiful butterfly. Much as God works inside our hearts to make each of us a new person in Christ.

Note the changes happening inside the chrysalis. Just as when we grow in Christ, people begin to see a change in us.

The butterfly develops inside the chrysalis.

Spreading Its Wings

After a time of struggling,
the butterfly is free to fly. Born again!

As we ask God into our hearts, we too are born
again and become new creatures in Christ.

To *die* to *self* is to become a new creature
in Christ. As the caterpillar dies to itself,
it becomes a new creature. Born again!

IN REPLY JESUS DECLARED,
"I TELL YOU THE TRUTH, NO ONE CAN SEE
THE KINGDOM OF GOD UNLESS HE IS BORN AGAIN."

JOHN 3:3

As the newborn butterfly struggles to emerge from the chrysalis, it becomes strong enough to fly. We also have struggles in our lives that make us strong in Christ.

The butterfly is now free to fly . . .
to go forth and lay many eggs
that will produce more caterpillars.
And each of them, too, will be born again
into new creatures.

Just as we are commanded to go forth as
disciples and help bring others to Christ.

THEREFORE GO AND MAKE DISCIPLES OF ALL
NATIONS, BAPTIZING THEM IN THE NAME OF THE
FATHER AND OF THE SON AND OF THE HOLY SPIRIT.

MATTHEW 28:19

A Beautiful Butterfly

Once there was a very ugly caterpillar.
All it wanted to do was eat and eat.
It thought it was pretty, so strong and so neat.

One day it spotted a lovely butterfly,
with its wings expanded wide.
"I'll be lovely too," it thought,
and began to gorge the leaves at its side.

It did nothing but eat and soon grew tired,
it decided to rest and the caterpillar expired.

It shed its skin; it turned short, fat, and green,
A sight to behold—it had to be seen.

One day it emerged all wrinkled and wet.
It hung upside down, so calm, without fret.
It began to move! Its wings were now dry.
It developed into a beautiful butterfly.

Creating your Own Butterfly Story

If you would like to have a hands-on experience of God's miracle–
the transformation of the hungry caterpillar into a beautiful born-again butterfly–
the following pages will help you get started.

Getting Started

There are two categories of plants that are necessary for butterfly gardening: nectar plants and host plants. Nectar plants, which are a source of food, attract adult butterflies. On host plants, female butterflies lay their eggs. They bend their abdomens and deposit the tiny eggs one at a time on the leaves. Monarch butterflies usually lay them on the underside of the leaves.

The eggs are round, creamy-white in color, and very tiny—as small as the head of a pin. You can watch the eggs hatch into tiny caterpillars, usually within four to seven days. Different species of butterflies like to lay their eggs on different types of host plants. When the eggs hatch, the caterpillars will feed on the leaves of the host plant.

When planting your butterfly garden, start small. You can expand it later, if you desire. Container plants—those grown in pots—do very well.

Attracting the Monarch

Let's attract the monarch—one of the most beautiful and colorful butterfly species. Popular throughout the United States, monarchs are relatively easy to attract and raise. They also live long, about eight months or more. Their host plant is the milkweed. (Another beautiful butterfly species, the black swallowtail, is also a good choice for your garden. Parsley is its host plant.)

Nectar Plants

Nectar plants, such as pentas, verbena, and lantana, feed adult butterflies. Another choice is the "butterfly bush" (*Buddleia*). You can grow one variety or a few. They will attract butterflies to your garden quickly– usually from a single day to a few weeks. All should be available at your local nursery or garden center.

Plant nectar plants in twelve-inch flowerpots or a flower bed that gets full sunlight for most of the day. Nurture with proper watering and plant food.

Host Plants

Plant the milkweed–host plant for the monarch–in another twelve-inch flowerpot or the flower garden. Start with one plant, adding more as the garden grows. Host plants should be located near nectar plants.

Pink Pentas

Pink Verbena

Yellow Lantana

Scarlet Milkweed

Create an Indoor Butterfly Habitat

Once you have planted the nectar and host plants in your garden, the butterflies will grow and flourish. You can also raise butterflies indoors (I do this on my back porch). All it takes are a few easily obtainable materials and a minimum amount of work.

SUPPLIES TO HAVE ON HAND

Large jar with a cover. A two- to four-quart glass or plastic container is recommended. A large may-

onnaise or pickle jar is a good choice, but any similar-sized container that you can see through will work just as well. I have even used a large goldfish bowl (minus the fish, of course). I covered the bowl with screening, which I secured with an elastic band.

Plastic containers are preferred as they are less likely to break, but any see-through container with a cover is fine.

You will have to make a number of small holes (around sixteen to twenty) in the cover to allow for sufficient air circulation. You can use a small nail or drill to make the holes.

Two small containers. Plastic film canisters with lids (the type that contains ordinary rolls of 35-millimeter film) are perfect. You can also use *thoroughly cleaned* pill bottles. In the center of each lid, make a hole that is big enough to fit a stem from the host plant.

Double-sided sticky tape. Only a short length of this tape is needed. You can purchase it at any stationery store.

A stem from the host plant. This stem must contain a few leaves and at least one caterpillar.

PUTTING IT TOGETHER

Once you have all the materials, it's time to "put it all together." To begin, fill one of the film canisters with water and put its lid (with the hole) back on. Secure it to the bottom of the large jar with a piece of double-sided tape.

Insert a stem from the host plant (with leaves and at least one caterpillar) into the canister through the hole in the lid. Place the cover back on the large jar. Remember, caterpillars are born to eat night and day. *Do not let yours run out of food.* As your caterpillar grows, it can eat up to five or six leaves a day!

Be sure to change the food supply as needed. To do this, remove the food canister from the jar–with the caterpillar still on the leaves–and place it on a table in your work area. Have the second food canister ready with a fresh stem from the host plant, and secure it to the bottom of the jar. Remove the stem

Secured in a large jar, a small film canister holds caterpillars and their food source.

(with the caterpillar) from the first canister and lay it on the bottom of the jar. The caterpillar will eventually find its way to the fresh food supply.

Be sure the large jar is always clean and dry. If it gets really dirty, wash it in hot soapy water, then rinse and dry it thoroughly before adding fresh food. You may have to do this every few days as the caterpillar gets bigger. It is okay to gently pick up larger caterpillars. They won't bite!

The caterpillar will eat and grow for two to three weeks. During this time, it will rest between growth spurts and shed its skin four times. After crawling out of its skin, the caterpillar may eat it. When it rests, it may do so on the top or side of the jar, or on a stick, which you can place in the jar. Before its final shedding, the caterpillar will go into a "J" shape and rest. It will attach itself to a stem, stick, or side of the jar, and shed its skin one last time.

A monarch caterpillar
enjoys a milkweed home.

A caterpillar just hours
before it becomes a pupa.

Nature's Royalty

After the caterpillar sheds its skin for the final time, it will change into a soft pupa, which will slowly become a chrysalis. As you can see from the photograph on the right, the chrysalis is green in color and has a black line that is trimmed in beautiful gold, like a crown. Small gold spots will also appear on the bottom of the chrysalis. Monarchs are considered the kings and queens of the butterflies. Many people believe that God has given the monarch chrysalis this gold crown to signify its "royalty."

THEREFORE IF ANY MAN IS IN CHRIST, HE IS A NEW CREATURE; THE OLD THINGS HAVE PASSED AWAY, BEHOLD NEW THINGS HAVE COME.

2 CORINTHIANS 5:17

The developing chrysalis.

Before your Eyes

In about ten days, the chrysalis will appear to turn black. But a closer look will surprise you. You can actually see the color of the new butterfly's wings inside the chrysalis. Within hours, it will hatch into a beautiful orange and black monarch butterfly. The monarchs almost always hatch in the morning, as the day begins. For as Psalm 30:5c tells us:

REJOICING COMES IN THE MORNING.
PSALMS 30:5c

And I rejoice every time one is born.

The butterfly starts to emerge from its chrysalis.

The butterfly frees itself from its shell.

Almost There...

When the newborn butterfly emerges, it hangs onto the empty chrysalis until its wings are dry. This generally takes from two to three hours. The butterfly is then ready to fly.

Always release butterflies when their wings are dry, so they may go forth to produce more eggs and create more lovely butterflies. If you put your finger directly under the new butterfly's nose/head, it will walk onto your finger. You can then walk it outside to a flower. This is very thrilling, especially for children!

There are many books on butterflies in bookstores and libraries that will expand your knowledge of this magnificent creature that our Father, the King of Creation, has given us to enjoy.

Happy
butterfly
gardening!

About the Author

Lucille Deith

The youngest of seven children, Lucille Deith was brought up on a small family farm. She always loved and chased after butterflies and fireflies, and had her own flower garden. She is an "ordinary, blessed" mother and grandmother —her daughter and granddaughter are true gifts of God.

Lucille is retired now, but she does a lot of volunteer work at her church. She gives "butterfly presentations" at the church school, ladies' groups, senior homes, and the like. Using a slide show along with scriptural passages, Lucille explains the growth process of the butterfly. For the children, she leaves a setup of one to two caterpillars and food plants. The children are excited to feed the caterpillars and watch them grow, until they are "born again" into beautiful butterflies.

Lucille Deith has a large garden designed to attract butterflies and she raises a number of different species there. She continually searches for new plants to attract new types of butterflies.

A caterpillar no more
as you flutter by,
Born again,
a butterfly.